PORTLAND OREGON

A PHOTOGRAPHIC PORTRAIT

Photography by

Susan E. Frost

First published in the United States
of America by:

Twin Lights Publishers, Inc.
8 Hale Street
Rockport, Massachusetts 01966
Telephone: (978) 546-7398
http://www.twinlightspub.com

ISBN: 1-885435-66-5
ISBN: 978-1885435-66-8

10 9 8 7 6 5 4 3 2 1

Editorial researched and written by
Susan E. Frost

Book design by
SYP Design & Production, Inc.
http://www.sypdesign.com

Printed in China

FREMONT BRIDGE (opposite)

The double-decked, Fremont Bridge is America's longest tied-
arch bridge at 1,255 feet. Built in 1973, it is Portland's newest
bridge. Lifting the magnificent arch's 6,000 tons into place
from the Willamette River set a world record. The bridge is
named after John Charles Fremont who surveyed the Oregon
Trail in 1842 and helped open the route to California from
The Dalles.

Welcome to Portland—the largest city in Oregon with half a million people within its borders and 1.6 million in the metropolitan area. The city is surrounded by hills, trees so tall they seem to touch the sky, and water, water everywhere. Fountains, rivers, ponds and plenty of rain keep the landscape green. It rains so much that Portlanders are sometimes referred to as "web foots".

Founded in 1845, Portland is relatively young compared to its east coast cousins. Named after Portland, Maine, the city is divided by Interstate 5 near the Washington and Oregon border, which is defined by the Columbia River. The growth of the city began in 1850 when it was a supply station for the California gold fields. The railroad's arrival in 1883, the 1897 Alaska gold rush, and the 1905 Lewis and Clark expedition fueled further growth.

Portland is often called the "City of Roses" because of its profusion of roses and its annual Grand Floral Parade. It is also called the "City of Bridges" because of the nine spans over the Willamette River that connect the east and west sides of the city.

Portland is a gateway to an outdoor wonderland, with the Willamette River winding through the center of the city and framed by Mount Hood. It is only 90 minutes by car to the pristine beaches along the Pacific coastline and one hour to fabulous skiing on Mount Hood. East of Portland on Interstate 84 is the Columbia River Gorge National Scenic Area, a geologic wonder of impressive cliffs, stunning views and numerous waterfalls including the 620-foot Multnomah Falls.

Over 37,000 urban parks and green spaces can be enjoyed within the Metro area. Tom McCall Waterfront Park, the most popular downtown park, extends along the west side of the Willamette River for over two miles. During the summer months, the park comes alive with numerous cultural and musical festivals.

In the northwestern hills of Portland, stroll through the Rose Gardens at Washington Park, a 100-acre treasure of over 8,000 roses, or take a meditative walk through the park's serene and beautiful Japanese Gardens.

Portland's downtown area is very accessible—no matter what form of transportation you choose—walking, biking, bus, light rail or streetcar within the 340-block "Fareless Square."

Walkers, bikers and joggers also have their own pathways throughout the metro area. Shortened downtown blocks, only 200 feet long, are lined with cafés, restaurants, bookstores, galleries and specialty stores. Fountains with bronze beavers, sea lions and bear cubs decorate the sidewalks.

In the center of downtown Portland is Pioneer Courthouse Square, a large public plaza sometimes called "Portland's living room." The square brings together a variety of representatives from the city's population, and becomes a cultural melting pot. On sunny summer days, a diverse lunch crowd gathers to listen to concerts or just enjoy time in the sun.

Let these 150 full-color photographs from *Portland, Oregon: A Photographic Portrait* walk you through this vibrant, eclectic and well-loved city.

SAILING MIGHTY COLUMBIA

Under full sail, a single sailboat glides on the Columbia River framed by majestic Mt. Hood and the I-205 Bridge. Sunny days in Portland encourage boat owners to sail or motor their boats on the Columbia River, a large expanse of water that provides a main water thoroughfare between Oregon and Washington.

HAWTHORNE BRIDGE AT DUSK *(top)*

The world's oldest vertical-lift bridge. Built in 1910, the Hawthorne Bridge connects the east and west side of Portland. In the early evening, soft lavender lights surround Portland's western skyline.

PIONEER COURTHOUSE SQUARE *(above and opposite)*

Pioneer Courthouse Square, in the center of downtown Portland, is known as Portland's living room. Each week, the brick plaza has a new display or event that attracts hundreds of people. On a sunny day, this square is a friendly place to eat lunch on the steps of the amphitheater or just sit and watch people go by.

AGNES FLANAGAN CHAPEL

Located at Lewis & Clark College and designed by architect,
Paul Thiry, the chapel's contemporary lines and conical shape
exhibit a Native American influence. The wooden figures
that flank the entrance to the chapel depict evangelists,
Matthew, Mark, Luke and John and were fashioned by Chief
Lelooska of the Cherokee tribe. Inside the chapel, which
seats 650 people, a beautiful Casavant organ with approxi-
mately 5,000 pipes is suspended from the ceiling.

CHERRY BLOSSOM TURN AROUND

Cherry trees bloom profusely during March along the Willamette River at the Tom McCall Waterfront Park. It is one of the most popular areas of Portland and hosts concerts and events year round. The esplanade, which parallels the entire length of the core downtown area, is frequented by walkers, joggers and bicyclists and is easily accessed by the downtown lunch crowd.

9

RIVERPLACE *(above)*

High-rise condominiums and sleek yachts define this area of Portland's urban harbor along the Willamette River.

ONE PACIFIC SQUARE *(opposite)*

Clouds are reflected on the shiny exterior of One Pacific Square, a 13-story, hexagonal glass building, that serves as the corporate headquarters for NW Natural Gas Company. Designed in 1983 by Yost Grube Hall Architecture, the building is located in Portland's Old Town section of the city.

VIEW OF CITY *(opposite)*

Mount Hood looms large over the city of Portland. This view
from the Pittock Mansion shows the density of downtown
buildings and mix of residences that extend close to
the base of Mount Hood.

TWIN TOWERS *(above)*

The twin glass towers of the Oregon Convention Center
(OCC) frame the eastern skyline of Portland. Located in the
Lloyd Center district, OCC is the largest convention center
in the Pacific Northwest at one million square feet on an
18-acre campus. Shown in the foreground are the Willamette
River and the East Bank Esplanade.

MARQUAM BRIDGE

The Marquam Bridge connects the west and east sides of
Portland. It is the busiest bridge in Oregon since all of the
main freeways in the area connect to this bridge. At 440 feet
in length, it is Oregon's first double-deck, vehicle-only bridge.

MOUNT HOOD RISES OVER PORTLAND

Like a ghostly apparition, Mount Hood appears to be suspended in air above Portland's downtown buildings. This view of the downtown area and Mount Hood was taken from Washington Park in the hills of western Portland.

QUIET AFTERNOON IN PORTLAND

This view of the Portland city skyline taken from the River
Place Amphitheatre, shows the downtown buildings facing
the Willamette River and the River Place Amphitheatre on a
rare, quiet day. Normally, this waterfront is filled with various
city events and boats cruising up and down the river.

SALMON SPRINGS FROLIC *(top)*

Children cool off by running through this popular downtown fountain on a hot summer day. Designed by Robert Perron, the fountain's three cycles and 185 jets change the outflow regularly to provide new water patterns, fondly referred to as, "mister", "bollards", and "wedding cake".

LIGHTS ON MORRISON BRIDGE *(bottom)*

A soft glow illuminates the Morrison Bridge which was the first of Portland's nine bridges to be lit as part of the Willamette Light Brigade's mission to light all of Portland's downtown bridges. The Morrison Bridge, originally built in 1887 and rebuilt in 1958, is Portland's oldest bridge.

SAILING DOWN RIVER

A colorful spinnaker propels a sailboat down the Columbia
River near the Portland Yacht Club. Sailing is a popular sport
among Portland residents during the summer months.

GLENN JACKSON BRIDGE

This two-mile-long bridge spans the Columbia River from Oregon to Washington and was built in 1977. Also referred to as the I-205 Bridge, because of freeway connections, vehicle traffic exceeds 125,000 per day. The twin structure with four lanes in each direction is unusual due to its nine-foot-wide bicycle and pedestrian path in the center of the bridge.

MEANDERING RIVER *(above)*

The Willamette River winds its way slowly through the fertile Willamette Valley near Portland, Oregon. Heavy rainfall, typically part of the Oregon climate, fills rivers and provides plenty of water for growing numerous crops. The Willamette Valley is known as Oregon's breadbasket for its ability to provide a wide abundance of food.

HOT AIR BALLOON RIDE *(opposite)*

A small group enjoys an early morning, hot air balloon ride over the peaceful Willamette River Valley. A popular pastime in the summer, hot air balloon provides the opportunity to drift slowly over the verdant fields and relish the awesome views.

NORTHWEST 23RD STREET (above)

Young people gather in front of the Everett Street Market in the Pearl District in Northwest Portland. This entire area used to be filled with old industrial warehouses. Now, "The Pearl" buzzes with creative activity as a result of its many trendy restaurants, breweries, shops, lofts and condominiums.

FLATIRON BUILDING (opposite)

Located at Stark and West Burnside Streets, the historic, narrow Flatiron Building was built in 1917 and served the automotive industry for many years. Today the landmark building houses Ringlers, a restaurant and bar owned by McMenamin Brothers, proprietors of several restaurants and breweries in Portland.

TWIST RETAIL STORE *(opposite)*

This brightly colored retail store, Twist, can be found just off West Burnside in the Pearl District. TVA Architects Inc. designed the building to visually adapt to a variety of uses including a gallery and specialty retail store.

EVENING SKYLINE REFLECTION *(above)*

Hues of reds and golds ripple across the Willamette River as it reflects the night lights of downtown Portland.

COTTON CANDY (above)

A nighttime view of the Ira C. Keller waterfalls provides an oasis of visual delights for event and concert attendees across the street at the Keller Auditorium. Designed by Lawrence Halprin, it was originally called the Forecourt Fountain. The name was changed in 1978 to honor Ira C. Keller, a visionary who contributed to urban renewal in Portland.

PORTLAND PLAZA (opposite)

Dots of light shine from Portland Plaza's interior while below, water streams like spun gold over the large granite blocks of the Ira Keller Fountains. This contemporary, high-rise glass wall condominium offers spectacular day or evening views of the city and is within walking distance of the Ira Keller Auditorium where Broadway shows and concerts are held.

IRA KELLER FOUNTAIN *(above)*

The Ira Keller Fountain with its beautiful cascading waterfalls beside thick, green trees and foliage, provide an inviting place for downtown office workers to bring their lunch and get away from the hectic pace of work.

WATERFRONT EXPLANADE *(opposite)*

The Tom McCall Waterfront Park with its mile-long esplanade along the seawall of the Willamette River is popular with joggers, pedestrians and in-line skaters. The park is home to many annual events, including the Portland Rose Festival, the Oregon Brewers Festival, and the Waterfront Blues Festival.

ALBERS MILL (*opposite*)

View of the Willamette River and the Fremont Bridge from the walkway behind Albers Mill, which used to be the largest cereal and grain manufacturing corporation on the Pacific Coast. Renovated in 1989, the building is now home to numerous businesses.

WILLAMETTE FALLS (*above*)

The 40-foot-high Willamette Falls at Oregon City, south of Portland, is one of the most visited and scenic spots in the area. It can be seen from several turnouts by driving east on the I-205 freeway. A series of locks was built in the early 1870's to allow safer travel for boats making the journey between Portland and the river cities in the Willamette Valley.

STEEL BRIDGE (top)

View of the Willamette River and Steel Bridge. It is the only double-deck bridge with independent lifts in the world and the second oldest vertical lift bridge in North America. It carries railroad and pedestrian traffic on the lower deck, with the MAX light rail and the Portland streetcar on the upper deck, which makes it one of the most multimodal bridges in the world.

ROSE GARDEN ARENA (bottom)

Home of the Oregon's NBA basketball team, the Trail Blazers, the Rose Garden is a 785,000-square-foot, multi-purpose facility which hosts a variety of sporting events including professional hockey, indoor track and field, and gymnastics. It also hosts major concerts, monster truck rallies, rodeo and bull riding, circuses, ice shows, boxing and convention and trade shows.

ST. JOHNS BRIDGE (opposite)

The Gothic Tower shown here is one of two, 408-foot-tall towers on the St. Johns Bridge which spans the Willamette River between the St. Johns neighborhood and the northwest industrial area around Linnton. The only suspension bridge in Portland, it was the longest rope-strand suspension bridge in the world at its time of construction in 1931.

HAWTHORNE BRIDGE *(above)*

Built in 1910, the Hawthorne Bridge has gained national recognition for its design. The oldest vertical-lift bridge in the world, it has been newly renovated and at night its brightly lit structure guides people to and from downtown Portland.

FORECAST--DRIZZLE *(opposite)*

Each day at noon in Pioneer Square the weather is forecast by the Weather Machine. On this particular day, the Blue Heron appears and his presence signifies rain. If the weather forecast is stormy, a dragon appears and if sunny, a golden sun. The clever instrument also tells the temperature.

OREGON HISTORICAL SOCIETY *(above and opposite)*

Shown above are the 8-story high, "trompe l'oeil" murals
by Richard Haas that depict members of the Lewis and Clark
expedition. They appear three dimensional, but are actually
painted on the exterior of the building. The image on the
right gives a wider perspective of the Oregon Historical
Society which houses its museum, the OMS Press, and the
OMS Research Library.

OREGON HISTORICAL SOCIETY

INTERNATIONAL ROSE TEST GARDEN (*above and opposite*)

Intense colors of orange, red and purple roses extend in thick profusion to the gazebo in the "Gold Medal Garden" within the International Rose Test Garden at Washington Park. Numerous fountains provide additional elements of interest among the over 8000 rose bushes in these gardens.

AUTUMN ON MOUNT HOOD *(above)*

Fall colors of red and gold frame Mt. Hood. Just one hour from downtown Portland, Mt. Hood has an abundance of prime camping spots and hiking trails. Huckleberries line the trails near mountain streams during late August and early September.

INTERNATIONAL ROSE TEST GARDEN *(opposite)*

Established in 1917, the International Rose Test Garden is the oldest public rose test garden in the United States. With more than 8,000 roses, a large amphitheater, tennis courts, hiking trails, stunning views of Mount Hood and the city skyline, it is one of Portland's most impressive landmarks.

SWALLOWTAIL ON COSMOS *(above)*

This Giant Swallowtail butterfly (Papilio cresphontes) is
shown hovering lightly over cosmos blooms at the Oregon
Zoo's butterfly exhibit.

VERTICAL PERSPECTIVE *(above)*

Rows of yellow and purple tulips form a *"V"* at the Wooden Shoe Tulip Farm in Woodburn, Oregon, just south of Portland.

LOVELY PINK ROSE *(bottom)*

Light softly illuminates this beautiful pink rose. It is one of the more than 600 varieties of roses found at the International Rose Test Garden section of Washington Park.

APRICOT ROSE *(top)*

An apricot colored rose, just one of over 600 varieties of roses that can be found in the International Rose Test Garden.

RHODODENDRON CENTER *(bottom)*

Close-up view of the center of a pink rhododendron, a very common flowering bush that grows prolifically throughout the Pacific Northwest.

ROSE GARDEN AMPHITHEATER

This large amphitheater at the International Rose Test Garden within Washington Park in the southwest hills of Portland is a popular place to view concerts by big name entertainers, or simply stop to sit and reflect on the surrounding beauty.

COUPLE ENJOY WATERFRONT (top)

A young couple pauses on a sunny day to view the Willamette River, Ross Island Bridge, and the Portland skyline.

RED ROSE (bottom)

Luscious, red, rich textures and subtle fragrance define this rose from the International Rose Test Garden in Washington Park.

PASTORAL SETTING

Colorful, pink Rhododendrons frame this pastoral setting of
waterfalls and soft green ferns and mosses in the tranquil,
natural garden (Shukeiyen) at the Japanese Gardens. Located
in the west hills of Portland at Washington Park, the Garden
was designed by Professor Takuma Tono and opened to the
public in 1967.

GARDEN OF SOLACE

The Garden of Solace in the Vietnam Veterans Living
Memorial at the Hoyt Arboretum serves as a place to stop
and reflect on the lives lost and those forever changed by the
Vietnam War.

ews in Coquille was the flood of '69, during which a man trying to rescue stranded cattle was drowned. A Lakeview man at the Joseph Rodeo
n from his horse and killed. In one coastal community a young man shot the town policeman and then himself. But there were many happy
se years; all those "annual events" which so many places have: Amity's pancake breakfast, Redmond's Potato Festival, the Pendleton Round-Up,
d its hundredth year, the Oregon State Fair.

OOK	VIRGIL A. CALKINS JR.	JAMES R. WOODS	FLOYD J. CRAIGMYLE	RICHARD H. BRIGHT
AG	JIM C. PAGE	LAWRENCE D. GREEF	RUDY L. BALDON	DON E. STOCKTON JR.
NSON	DELOS R. BUXTON	LARRY J. WHEELER	DANIEL L. HART	RICHARD E. WESTFALL
MB	JOHN C. HANSEN	ROBERT F. MC CLAFLIN	CRAIG S. GREEN	WILLIAM R. CRANE
HNSON	ROBERT D. BUSWELL	MELVIN L. GRANT	ALLEN D. PERKINS	PATRICK A. CADWALLADER
ATON	STEPHEN D. GLECKLER	DARYL M. MOGCK	JERRY E. KEKEL	DAVID L. SMITH
RRELL	DAVID E. BRAMSEN	DAVID B. LENTZ	JOHN A. BOSSOM	GERALD R. WADE
ORNE	DANIEL A. IRELAN	JOHN E. WIBBENS	TIMOTHY E. ACHISON	EDWARD R. STORM
RSON	DAVID TORRES	ANTHONY B. BLAIR		
MSON	GEORGE S. DORMAN	JAMES E. MC WHORTER		
RSON	SAMUEL BETZ	DENNIS M. GILLERAN		
OM	LEVI L. ARMSTRONG	HERBERT C. HEINTZ		

1969

VIETNAM MEMORIAL WALL

This gracefully curved, black granite wall is just one of several
in the Vietnam Veterans Living Memorial that honors
Oregon soldiers dead or missing in action by year. The names
on these inscribed walls serve as a somber reminder of their
sacrifice.

FLOWERING CHERRY TREE *(above)*

Wispy, flowering branches from this cherry tree almost touch the walkway near Johns Landing on the Willamette River. Residents walk and jog on this pathway that is sandwiched between the Willamette River and residential and commercial buildings.

ARCHITECTURAL LINES *(opposite)*

This is one of the many contrasting views of the city of Portland from the International Rose Test Garden. The lines of the Frank L. Beach Memorial Fountain sculpture in the foreground seem to line up with the second largest skyscraper of Portland, the US Bancorp Tower. Portlanders fondly refer to this building as "Big Pink".

QUEEN'S COURT *(above)*

The 2005 Rose Festival Queen and her court grace Portland's Grand Floral Parade, which is the second largest floral parade in North America. As part of this event, one high school senior per school is chosen to join the Royal Court of Rosaria. From this court, the Queen is chosen.

TEDDY ROOSEVELT *(opposite)*

This statue of Teddy Roosevelt on horseback, in a Spanish-American war uniform, is called Theodore Roosevelt/Rough Rider. Sculptor Alexander Phimister Proctor was commissioned by Portland philanthropist, Henry Waldo Coe to create the monument. One of several statues of United States presidents donated to Portland by Coe, it stands proudly in the South Park Blocks in downtown Portland, between the Portland Art Museum and the Oregon History Center.

QUEST

The sculpture of the nude figures intertwined is called "Quest",
and was designed by Count Alexander Von Svoboda. It graces
the entrance to the Standard Insurance Center. Von Svoboda
described it thusly: "It depicts the growth of today and tomorrow
and the awakening to the future. I wanted to have complete
contrast between this piece of sculpture and the Georgia-Pacific
Building. The sculpture is designed to lead the beholder to look
towards the middle of the building and then up."

SOARING STONES

A group of granite stones perched on top of mirror-finished steel pedestals, gives the impression that the stones could come crashing down at any moment. Designed by John T. Young, this whimsical sculpture is across from Saks Fifth Avenue.

OLD AND NEW *(opposite)*

The old Portland sign from the Schnitzer Performing Arts Center stands in sharp contrast to the new, modern Fox Tower. Designed by TVA Architects Inc., this building is one of Portland's newest downtown office towers.

PORTLANDIA *(above)*

Portlandia, the beautiful, yet powerful sculpture of a woman, is 36 feet tall and the second-largest hammered copper statue ever built. It was designed by Raymond Kaskey and sits above the entrance to the Portland Building, which was designed by Michael Graves.

DOWNTOWN JAIL *(opposite)*

The Multnomah County Justice Center is Portland's only downtown detention facility. From the outside, might appear to be an office building. With its beautiful exterior, retail shops and restaurant, Bob Frasca, chief designer from architecture firm, Zimmer Gunsul Frasca, once described the sleek, deceiving building as "perfuming the slammer".

CUSTOMS HOUSE *(above)*

The United States Customs House is a study in historic architectural detail, with its Roman arches and intricate detail dressing the exterior. The interior features opulent courtrooms that were never used. In 1974, the building was placed on the National Register of Historic Places and today is still one of Portland's finest buildings.

PITTOCK MANSION (*above*)

The Pittock Mansion is one of Portland's favorite landmarks. Visitors stroll on the 46-acre grounds to take in views of the Cascade Mountains. The mansion was owned by the founder of *The Oregonian*, Henry Louis Pittock, and as an historic monument, it is now a well-preserved testimony to a bygone era of romance and extravagance.

UNION STATION TOWER (*opposite*)

The Union Station tower has been a Portland landmark since 1893. Amtrak still provides daily stops, but the number of stops has diminished to less than half of the original 92 daily runs.

BRONZE BEAVERS (*above*)

The bronze sculptures of the beaver and his friends in the fountain are found along Yamhill Street next to the Pioneer Courthouse. The beaver is Oregon's official state animal. Other *Animals in Pools* sculptures, designed by Georgia Garber, include a mother and her two cubs, a doe and fawn and two river otters at various locations within the core area of downtown Portland.

ALLOW ME (*opposite*)

The ubiquitous Umbrella Man is raising his hand to signal a cab. This statue, called *Allow Me*, was designed by J. Seward Johnson and is one of 181 public sculptures in Portland. It holds a prominent place in Pioneer Courthouse Square and rain or shine, Portlanders and visitors love to be photographed with this statue.

THE PROMISED LAND *(above)*

Oregon was established by pioneers and this bronze statue of a pioneer family, called *The Promised Land*, designed by David Manuel, conveys their relief at reaching the end of the Oregon Trail. The statue is located in Chapman Square across from the Multnomah County Justice Center.

CAPTAIN WILLIAM CLARK MONUMENT *(opposite)*

Captain Clark looks out to the Willamette River from Waud's Bluff, the farthest known point reached by the explorers. Beside him is his black slave York and a Native American. The statues, sculpted by Michael Florin Dente, can be seen at the University of Portland.

MADE IN OREGON *(above)*

Cherry blossoms soften and surround the "Made in Oregon" sign located at the west end of the Broadway Bridge. The symbol of the white stag leaping is the only remaining indication that the sign used to represent White Stag skiwear and clothing beginning in 1929. Now, the White Stag label is owned by Wal-Mart, Inc.

WATERFRONT JOGGERS *(opposite)*

Springtime in Portland is synonymous with cherry blossoms. Along the esplanade of the Tom McCall Waterfront Park, joggers relish the sunny day. The Twin Towers of the Oregon Convention Center can be seen across the Willamette River.

BURNSIDE BRIDGE PILLAR (opposite)

The Italian Renaissance tower is one of two artistically-designed towers on the historic Burnside Bridge. The grand piers sit on timber pilings and are topped with turrets for the bridge operator to see up and down the river. The 2,308-foot bridge is an excellent vantage point for attendees of the Rose Festival Parade and a perfect spot to photograph the Willamette River.

BLUES AND BOATS (above)

Tom McCall Waterfront Park during Fourth of July weekend is host to more than 120,000 blues fans who gather by boat or stretch out on the lawn to hear performances by over 100 blues artists on four stages. It is the largest blues festival west of the Mississippi.

MULTNOMAH VILLAGE (*above*)

This colorful window display is that of Birdie's specialty retail shop in Multnomah Village, which is one of 95 officially recognized Portland neighborhoods.

BLAGEN BLOCK (*opposite*)

Built in 1888, the Blagen Block Building is an excellent example of the ornate cast-iron facades that appeared on nearly all the buildings in this area at one time. It is located in Old Town at 78 NW Couch. The MAX light rail train goes by here regularly and Portland's Saturday Market is next door.

URBAN PARK (*top*)

A father and his two daughters stop to swing and enjoy one of the many small, urban parks within the downtown Portland area.

PGE PARK (*bottom*)

Recently renovated PGE Park, (formerly the Civic Stadium) is Portland's athletic stadium that hosts baseball, soccer, and football. The old-fashioned ballpark seats 23,150 people. Roman arches in the front are preserved with a great color scheme. The wire sculpture of the man's head adds a touch of humor.

JOAN OF ARC (*opposite*)

This glistening gold statue of Joan of Arc, which recently underwent gilding and restoration, was dedicated in 1925 to commemorate U.S. soldiers who fought in France during World War I. It is located near Laurelhurst Park at the Coe Circle turnaround at Burnside and 39th Avenue.

JOAN OF ARC

UNIVERSITY CLUB (*above*)

Strategically located near the pulse of downtown Portland, the historic University Club was founded in 1898 for men only by a group of Ivy League college graduates. In 1903, the club began admitting women and now serves as a catalyst for fellowship and a gathering place for both male and female members.

UNIVERSITY OF PORTLAND (*opposite*)

Rhododendrons bloom near the brick tower of Waldschmidt Hall, the administration building, at the University of Portland. The architecture is classic Richarsonian Romanesque which was popular in the late 19th century.

FIRST CONGREGATIONAL CHURCH *(above)*

The dramatic 175-foot, cream and red latticed tower is that of the First Congregational Church, one of the few remaining Venetian Gothic style buildings in Portland. Dedicated in 1895, it continues to be an elegant presence in the South Park Blocks. The building on the right is the Arlene Schnitzer Hall, part of the Portland Center for the Performing Arts complex.

MILE POST SIGN *(opposite)*

Take your pick. Distances to Portland's nine sister cities and other geographical destinations are listed on this whimsical signpost.

LIGHT RAIL STATION

The underground tunnel for Portland's light rail train called
MAX (Metropolitan Area Express), is the deepest under-
ground transit station in North America. Artwork at the
Washington Park Station includes murals and rock tubes that
outline millions of years of geological development in the
West Hills.

PORTLAND INTERNATIONAL AIRPORT

The sky bridge entrance to Portland International Airport
is just 20 minutes from downtown Portland. It is one of the
nation's most pleasant and easily accessible airports—with
plenty of shops, restaurants and conference centers available
for the traveler on the run. Sixteen airlines serve PDX
with direct and non-stop service to more than 100 cities
worldwide.

WORLD TRADE CENTER (left)

Portland's World Trade Center is a hub for international businesses and conferences. Located directly across from Tom McCall Waterfront Park, it is within walking distance of major businesses, financial institutions, government offices and restaurants.

UPTOWN SHOPPING CENTER (right)

This covered walkway is part of the Uptown Shopping center in the Nob Hill district in fashionable Northwest Portland. This area is surrounded by elegant mansions. Many of these surviving homes are filled with boutiques and restaurants.

ARCHWAY TO NORDSTROMS (opposite)

This glass skylight with its diffused illumination leads into Nordstrom's, one of the anchor tenants for Lloyd Center Mall in northeast Portland. Built in 1960, the three-level urban mall, with over 200 stores and 1.5 million square feet, is the largest mall and business center in Oregon.

QUEEN'S WALKWAY (*opposite*)

The names of each Portland Rose Festival Queen are etched onto bronze plaques that dot the brick pathway leading into the Shakespeare Garden. The Shakespeare Garden is located within the International Rose Festival Garden at Washington Park.

WORLD FORESTRY CENTER (*above*)

The entrance to the Discovery Museum in the World Forestry Center at Washington Park welcomes patrons with light and color. The 20,000-square-foot museum has been recently renovated. The new hands-on, interactive exhibits are family-friendly and designed to engage visitors to learn about the sustainability of forests of the Pacific Northwest and the world.

ROYAL ROSARIAN AND BAND (top)

A member of the Royal Rosarians smiles as he marches in
the Grand Floral Parade along with the high school band
trumpet players. The Royal Rosarians have served as ambas-
sadors of goodwill for the City of Roses since 1912.

MANY HUES (bottom)

Colorful crayons decorate this float in Portland's Grand
Floral parade, the second largest all-floral parade in North
America. It is also the largest spectator event in Oregon,
drawing a crowd of over half a million people along a 4.3
mile route.

STRUTTING LLAMAS

High-stepping llamas proudly strut for the crowd at the
Grand Floral Parade. After 11 years marching in the parade,
the llamas know what to expect and enjoy showing off.

OMSI *(top)*

The Oregon Museum of Science and Industry (OMSI), one of the top 10 science museums in the United States, has five exhibit halls and eight science labs that extend 219,000 square feet. OMSI features a big screen OMNIMAX Theater, the Pacific Northwest's largest planetarium and the USS Blueback submarine exhibit.

INVENTOR'S BALL ROOM *(bottom)*

A brightly-colored ball catcher at OMSI's Inventor's Ball Room is featured in an interactive exhibit where visitors can design systems to transport balls and, in the process, learn about physics, problem solving, and engineering.

INNOVATION STATION *(opposite)*

Visitors find many opportunities to invent, build, experiment, and discover what happens when science and fun come together at OMSI's Innovation Station.

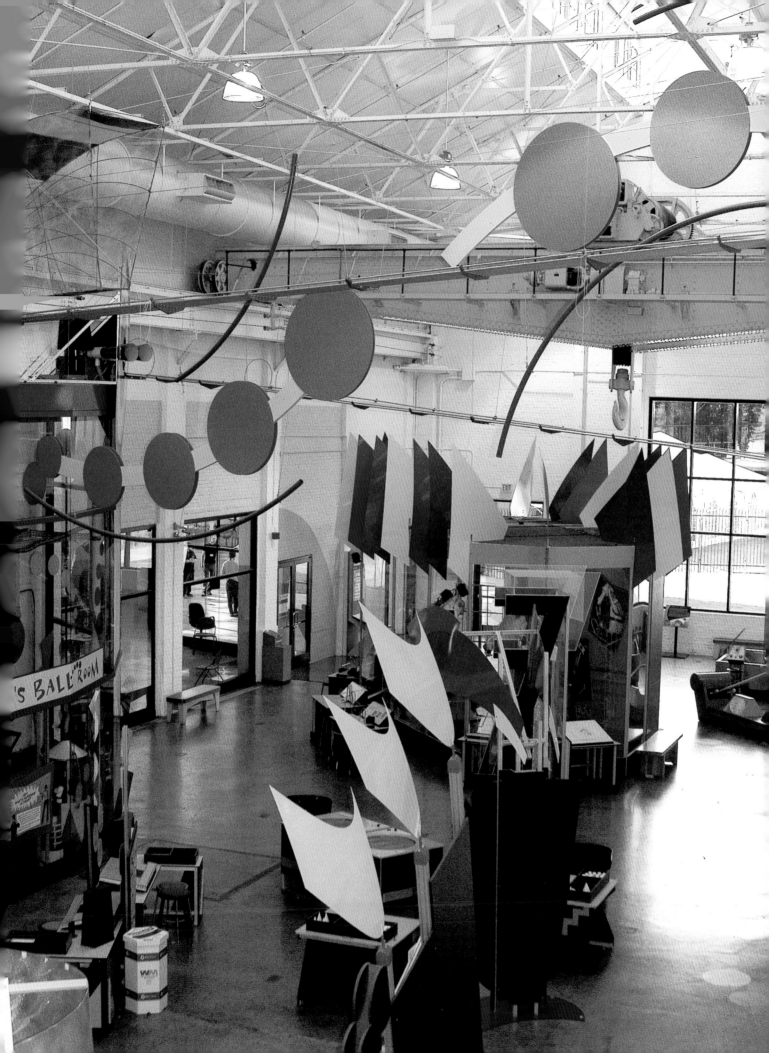

HEATHMAN HOTEL STAIRWAY *(left)*

Stairway to the mezzanine at the Heathman Hotel, one
Portland's finest boutique hotels in downtown Portland.
A four-star hotel with an award-winning restaurant, it is a
popular destination for tourists and business travelers.

HEATHMAN CHANDELIER *(right)*

This Austrian hand-cut crystal chandelier casts a soft glow on
the historic Tea Court in the Heathman Hotel. Contemporary
art exhibits brighten the mezzanine, which serves as an
entrance to the banquet and meeting rooms.

GREEK ORTHODOX CHURCH

Interior of the sanctuary at the Holy Trinity Greek Orthodox Church in Northeast Portland. The church is known for their annual Greek Festival in October that celebrates Greek traditions with music, dancing and homemade food.

ROCKY BUTTE PANORAMA

Red lava gravel forms a 360-degree path around the perimeter of Joseph Wood Hill Park at Rocky Butte Natural Area in Northeast Portland. Known for its stunning panoramic views, Rocky Butte is one of more than 50 vents and cones of the Boring Lava Field surrounding Portland.

STAIRWAY TO JOSEPH WOOD HILL PARK

Stone walls and a winding stairway lead to Joseph Wood Hill Park at Rocky Butte. The stone walls were put in by the Works Progress Administration from 1937 to 1939.

PIONEER WAGON WHEEL *(top)*

A wagon wheel, along with flour sacks and butter churn, are displayed in the Oregon Trail section of the *Oregon My Oregon*, a permanent exhibit at the Oregon Historical Society. The presentation depicts life as it was for pioneers who traveled to Oregon in the mid-1800s, including a replica of a store stocked with 1940s merchandise.

OREGON EXHIBIT *(bottom)*

Oregon's seal and flag, as well as the beaver and other representative icons, are part of the *Oregon My Oregon* Exhibit. The show occupies an entire floor and traces the history, geography and culture of Oregon through interactive displays, and two theaters.

OLD BOOTS *(opposite)*

Old boots, rumpled and worn, hang on display at a small grocery store outside Portland, Oregon.

ENTRANCE TO THE JAPANESE GARDEN *(top)*

This sign marks the entrance to the Japanese Garden in Portland's West Hills. One of the most authentic Japanese gardens outside of Japan, it is a haven of tranquil beauty with five formal gardens on five and one-half acres.

STAG LANTERN *(bottom)*

The finely carved granite lantern with a pagoda shaped roof is known as the Stag Lantern. The firebox has carvings of deer, snails and the full moon. It is one of many Asian treasures found at the beautiful Japanese Garden in Washington Park.

JAPANESE CHERRY TREE

The flowering Japanese Cherry tree extends its flower laden
branches over the Flat Garden during March. It is one of
many special botanicals in the Japanese Garden at
Washington Park. This landscape includes Shirakawa
Sand raked in careful patterns representing water.

MID-LAKE PAVILION

The Mid-Lake Pavilion at the Portland Classical Chinese
Garden is reflected in Lake Zither while water lilies float idly
by. An oasis designed to change with the seasons, it is never
the same twice.

RAINBOW BRIDGE

The Rainbow Bridge leads into the fragrant courtyard at the right. Strolling across Zither Lake, the covered bridge is just one of many serpentine walkways in the Garden of Awakening Orchids section of the Portland Classical Chinese Garden.

STONE MOSAIC (left)

Stone pebbles, in combination with bits of quarried stone, broken pottery, and roof tiles, are used throughout the Portland Classical Chinese Garden walkways and paved courtyards in a wide variety of patterns. Shown here is the Cross-Eight design.

MOON GATE (right)

"Listen to the fragrance as the garden unfolds before you", says the Chinese calligraphy above the entrance to the pebbled mosaic courtyard. Walking barefoot on the smooth pebbles gently massages the feet.

VIEW FROM THE TOP

A bird's eye view of the 40,000 square-foot, walled enclosure shows its elegant pavilions and ponds bordered by walkways and arched bridges. Lan Su Yuan, the Garden of Awakening Orchids, also known as the Classical Chinese Garden, was designed and constructed by architects and artisans from Suzhou, China as an authentic Ming Dynasty Scholar's garden, with tools that would have been used in the 14th century Ming Dynasty.

GUARDIAN LION (*above*)

This granite lion is one of two large stone guardians protecting the entrance plaza of the Portland Classical Chinese Garden.

CHINATOWN STREETLAMP (*opposite*)

One of 57 twin, ornate street lamps, painted red and gold, signifys good luck and prosperity. The Chinatown banners help to define the boundaries of this historic area, which covers an eight-block radius beginning at NW Fourth and Burnside.

華埠

CHINATOWN

A part of the
Old Town/Chinatown
Neighborhood

華埠

CHINATOWN

A part of the
Old Town/Chinatown
Neighborhood

URBAN WINE WORKS *(left)*

Stacks of painted wine barrels are found at Urban Wine Works in Northwest Portland. All of the wines are made by different Northwest vintners. One of Portland's favorite wine bars, this is a great place to sip and taste wine in a fun atmosphere.

PINOT NOIR CLUSTER *(right)*

A ripe, Pinot Noir grape cluster dangles from the vine of one of Oregon's vineyards near Portland. More Pinot Noir wine is produced each year in Oregon than any other variety, second to Pinot Gris. In 2004, 540,000 cases of Pinot Noir were sold. Oregon wines are popular both nationally and internationally.

REX HILLS VINEYARD (above)

This small section of the 20-acre, Rex Hill Estate Vineyard is located south of Portland. The Rex Hill winery is one of over 250 wineries in Oregon; many are within a 40 minute drive from Portland. The success and popularity of Oregon's wineries is partly attributed to the Willamette Valley's fertile soil and ideal growing conditions.

BEER TAPS *(above)*

Authentic beer tap stanchions from Germany made of
Majolica ceramic and brass are used to draw favorite beers for
patrons of MacTarnahans Tap Room at the Pyramid Brewery
in Northwest Portland. With 23 breweries within the city
limits and 34 breweries in the metro area, Portland now has
more craft brewers than any other city in the United States
and is considered one of the world's great brewing capitals.

COPPER VESSELS *(opposite)*

These two gigantic copper vessels are used to brew beer by
the Pyramid Brewery (formerly Portland Brewery) in Northwest Portland. The mash tun, (vessel nearest the tap room)
strains the hops and the kettle is used for boiling. The
coppers were built originally for a brewery in Germany.

USS BLUEBACK (above)

USS Blueback was the last non-nuclear powered submarine built by the U.S. Navy, and the last to be decommissioned after serving her country for 31 years. Named for the Sockeye Salmon or "Blueback", the 220-foot submarine was home to 90 sailors during the Cold War maneuvers and was used in the film "Hunt for Red October". The USS Blueback now makes its home at the Oregon Museum of Science and Industry (OMSI).

USS BLUEBACK PROPELLER (opposite)

Looking a bit like modern sculpture, the original screw propeller of the USS Blueback submarine is now part of the United States Submarine Memorial display at OMSI.

PORTLAND SUNRISE

Sunrise in Portland shines a bright path across the
Willamette River while a tugboat quietly pushes its barge
upriver toward the Hawthorne Bridge. Tugboats are routinely
used to transport large loads that other ships can't carry.

COLUMBIA SLOUGH *(top)*

The Island Café in the Columbia Slough is a great place for boats owners and houseboat residents to unwind on a summer day. The ever present ducks seek the leftovers from the restaurant patrons.

GOVERNOR KULONGOSKI *(bottom)*

Oregon Governor Ted Kulongoski proudly accepts a plaque displaying the newly minted, 2005 Oregon quarter from the Associate Director of the United States Mint, Gloria Eskridge.

PORTLAND STREETCAR

This sleek, Euro-designed streetcar is shown in the North Park Blocks near Portland State University. It is just one of several new streetcars that follow a six-mile loop and travel throughout downtown Portland, the Pearl District and the Northwest/Nob Hill neighborhood.

WESTSIDE MAX

The West Side MAX, is part of an electric transportation grid that extends 44 miles throughout the Portland Metro area. Transportation is easy in Portland—especially in Fareless Square. Just hop on a Tri-Met bus, MAX light rail or Portland Streetcar and it won't cost you a dime within a 330-block downtown radius.

TWO ELEPHANTS TALKING (*above*)

Asian Elephants named Sung Surin (right) and Rose Tu (left) appear to be carrying on a conversation at the Oregon Zoo within Portland's Washington Park. This zoo is recognized internationally for having the most successful breeding herd of Asian elephants of any zoo. Since 1962, 27 calves have been born at the Oregon zoo.

BALD EAGLE IN FLIGHT (*opposite*)

This magnificent Great Bald Eagle with his 8-foot wing span, can be seen up close at the new Eagle Canyon exhibit at the Oregon Zoo. Each year, over one million visitors wander the zoo's 64-acres that are home to animals and birds from all corners of the world.

MRS. CHIMP *(above)*

Female chimpanzee, Deliah, lives with her family, Coco and Leah, in one of the Oregon Zoo's oldest exhibits. The zoo has participated in species survival plans and international breeding programs for these endangered animals.

LORIKEET *(opposite)*

Bright oranges, yellows and greens make this Swainson's Lorikeet stand out at the Lorikeet Landing exhibit in an enclosed aviary with over 90 Lorikeets. Visitors can hand-feed these beautiful and friendly parrots. The Oregon Zoo has been very successful in breeding rare birds.

AMUR LEOPARDS *(above)*

Frederick is one of two critically endangered Amur leopards. With only 50 left in the wild, the zoo draws attention to the plight of these beautiful cats. Currently, Amur leopards can only be found in a small area along the Russian and Chinese border, overlapping the much larger range of the Siberian tiger.

HERON TAKE-OFF *(opposite)*

A great blue heron, Portland's official bird, spreads his 6-foot wingspan in flight at the Oaks Bottom Wildlife Refuge in Southeast Portland. These 160-acre wetlands are home to numerous great blue herons, coots, mallards, pintails, hawks and many other birds that can be seen by just strolling along the paved trails.

WATERFRONT VILLAGE

A crescent moon, a brightly lit Ferris wheel, and lights from
thrill rides reflected in the Willamette River all add to the
enjoyment of the Pepsi Waterfront Festival. This 11-day Rose
Festival event, at the Tom McCall Waterfront Park, draws
more than 375,000 visitors each year to experience entertain-
ment, concessions and rides along the Willamette River.

OREGON SYMPHONY

Music Director, Carlos Kalmar, conducts the Oregon
Symphony at the Arlene Schnitzer Concert Hall. Established
over 100 years ago, the Oregon Symphony is internationally
renowned. Comprised of 88 full-time musicians, the ORS is
one of the largest orchestras in the nation, with an annual
attendance of more than 320,000.

AUTUMN IN PORTLAND *(above and opposite)*

September is one of the prettiest times to visit Portland. Weather is warm, and the leaves on the deciduous trees turn from plain green to rich hues of gold, yellow and orange.

WINTER FOG

Pale shades of grey fog surround bare trees creating winter silhouettes. Cold, wet and foggy scenes like this are typical in Portland during the winter.

GREY DAY IN PORTLAND *(above)*

Portland has more grey days of rain and clouds than sunshine. This is a winter view of the Willamette River, downtown Portland, Tom McCall Waterfront Park and the Hawthorne Bridge.

SPRING RUN-OFF *(page 128)*

Nothing is more inviting than sunshine on a late spring day in Oregon. This view of Mount Hood shows the Salmon River in the foreground.